THIS COLORING BOOK BELONGS TO:

COPYRIGHT 2020 EDFRABEL COLORING BOOKS
AUTHOR ,ILLUSTRATOR OR PUBLISHING INFO:
EDFRABEL@GMAIL.COM

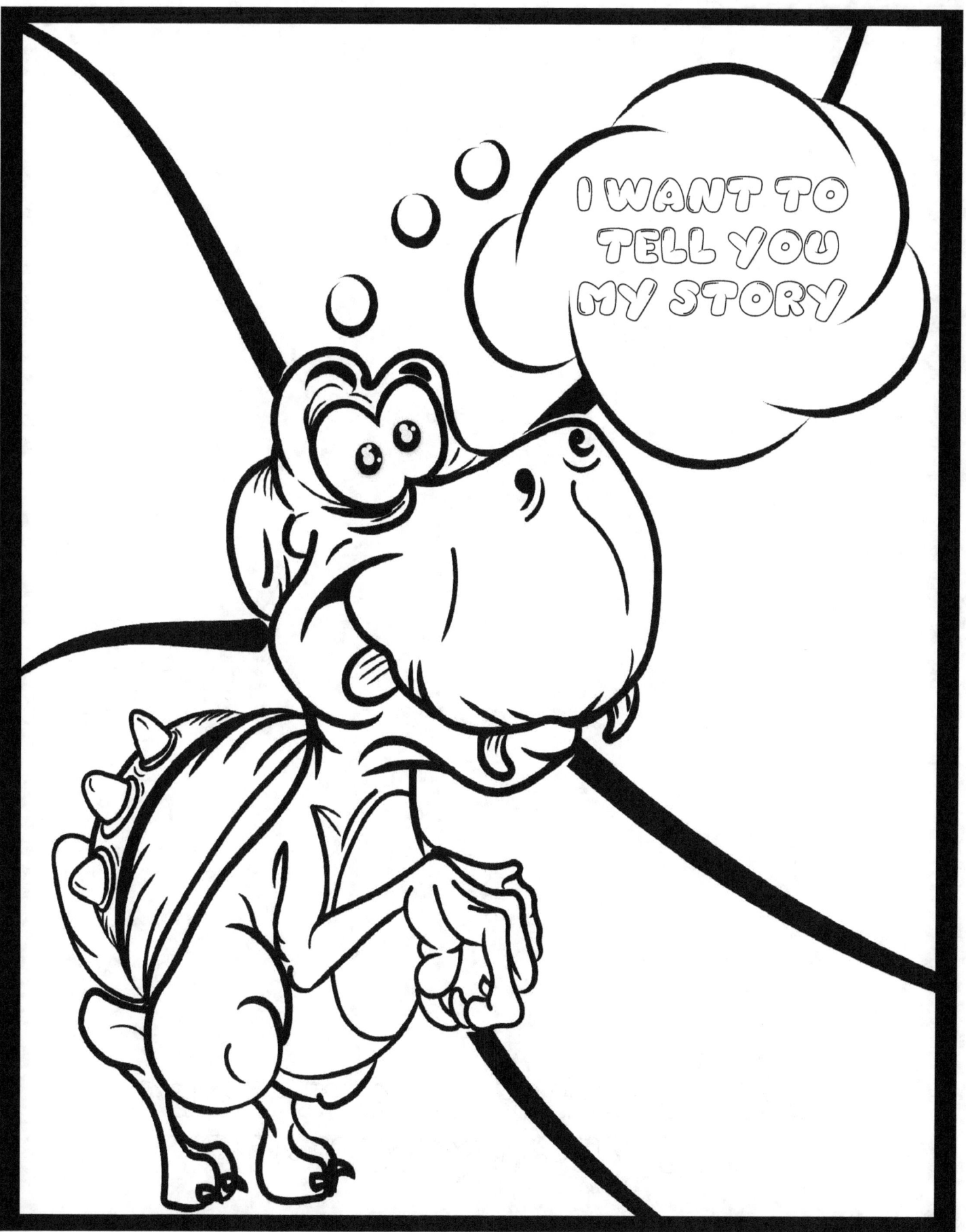

ABOUT WHAT I HAVE TO DO FOR GET MY DONUTS

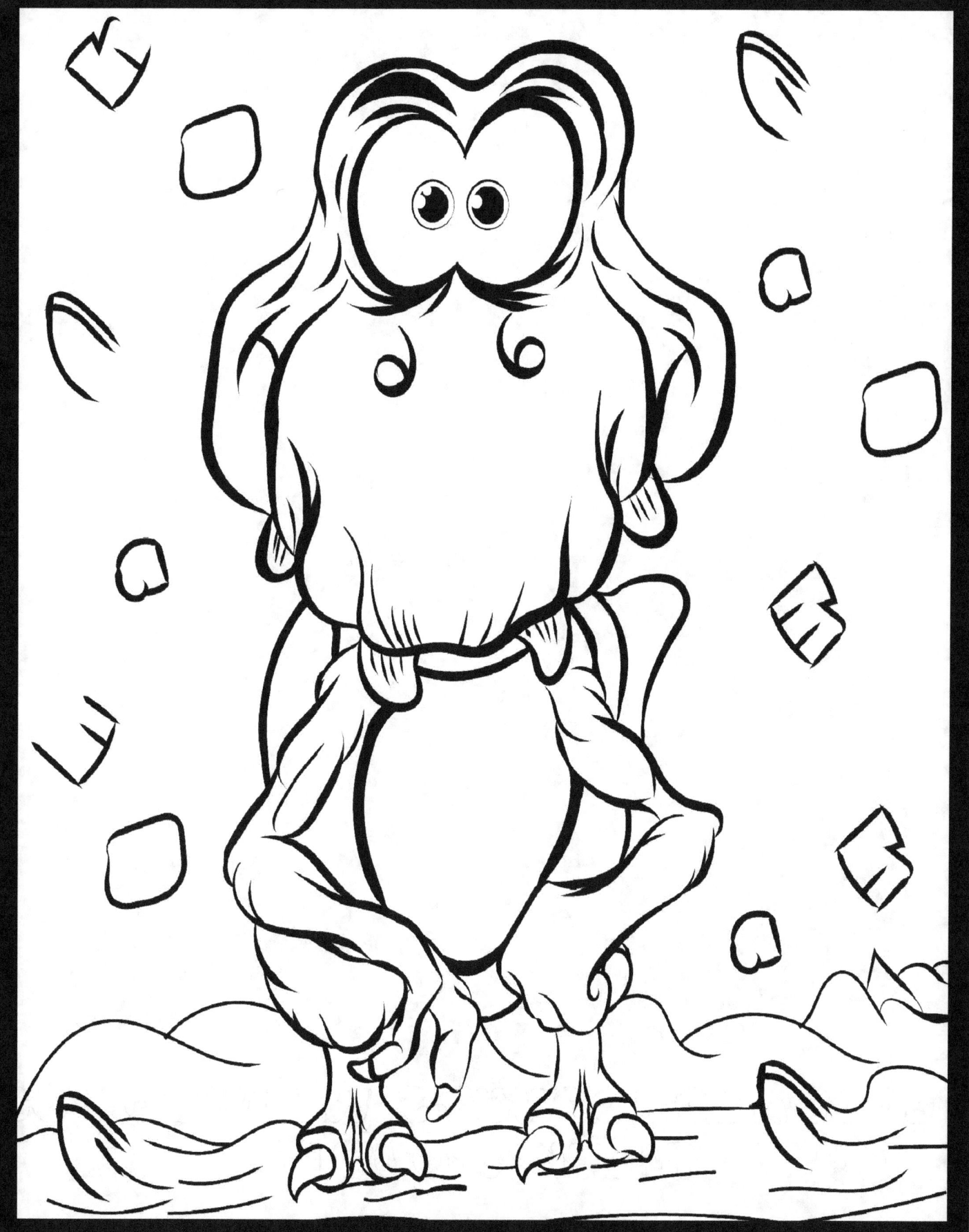

I LOVE A LOT DONUTS, WHAT DO YOU THINK ABOUT IT.

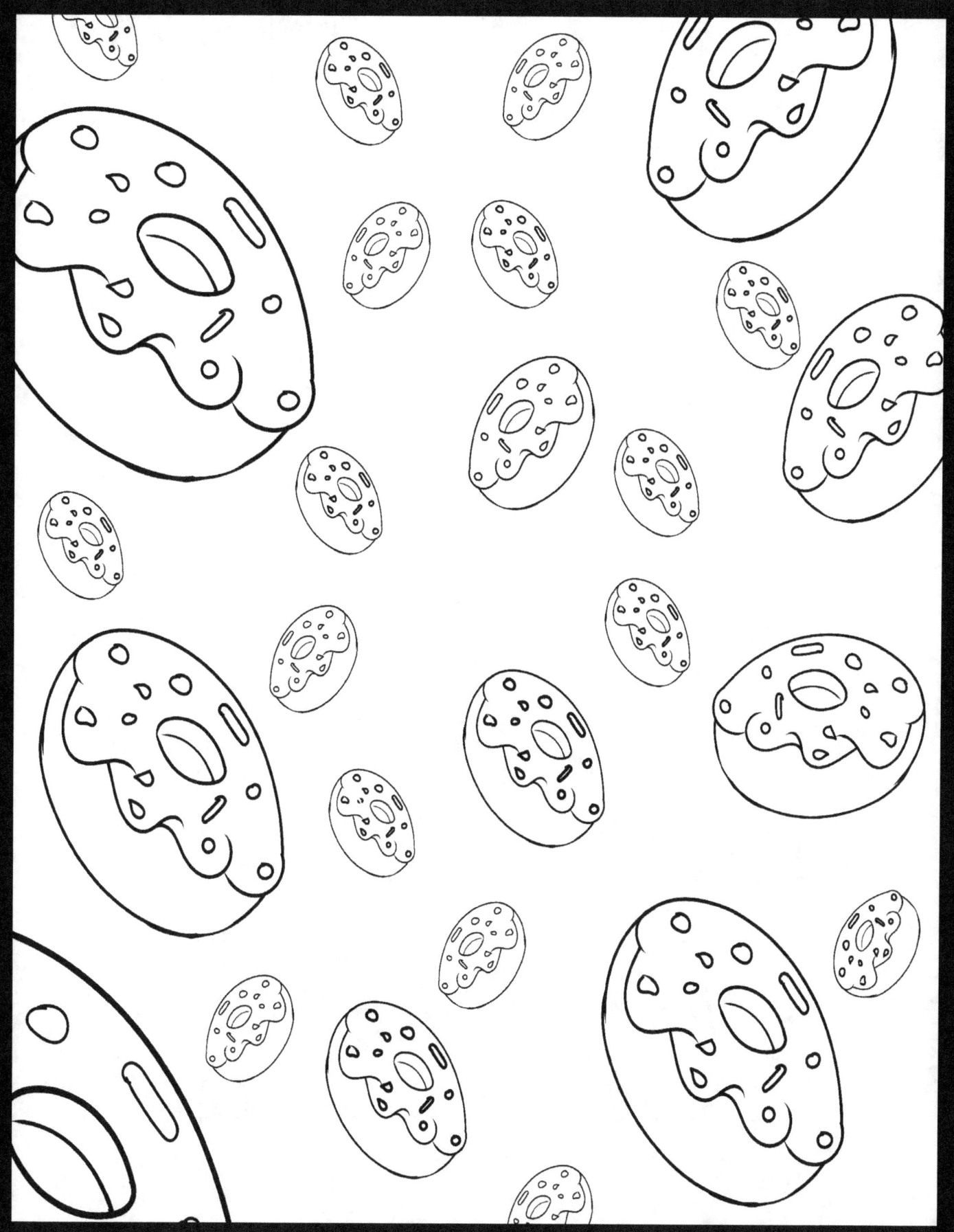

I LOVE CAKES AS WELL.

THATS WHAT I HAVE ALWAYS
DREAMED GO TO
THE DOUNT PLANET

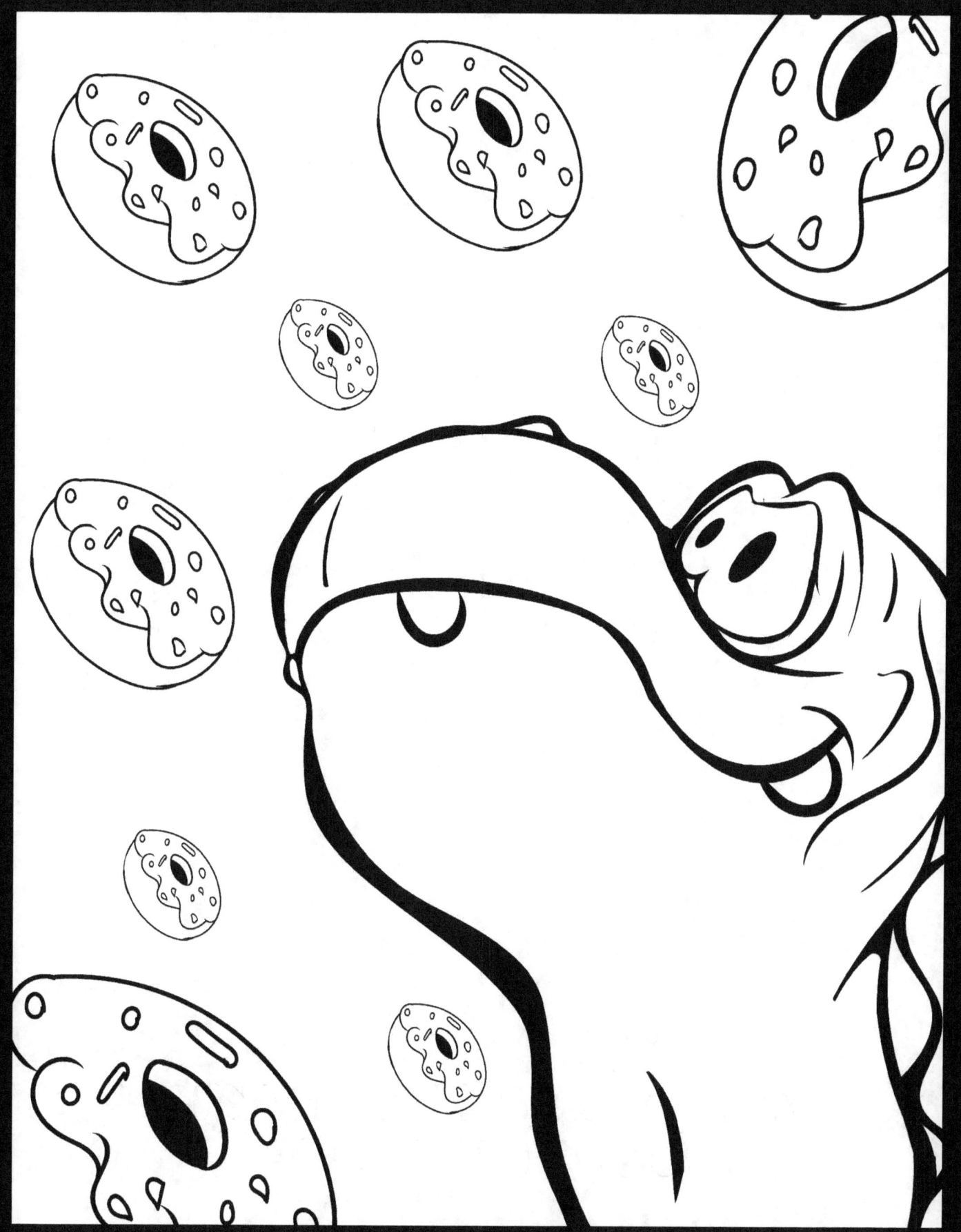

AND I CAN NOT THINK IN
ANYTHING ELSE.

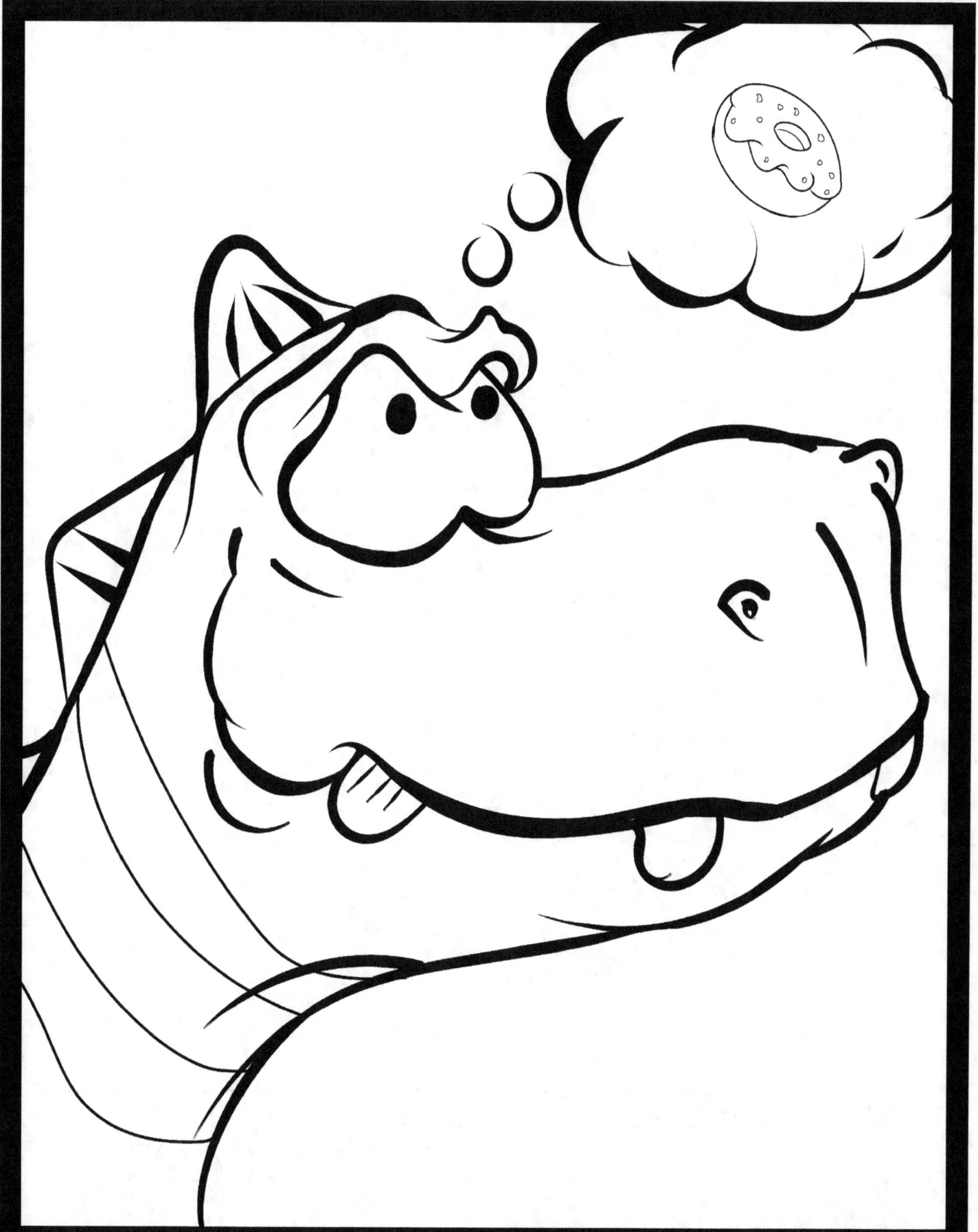

SO I DECIDED TO GO THERE, EVEN IT IS TOO FAR FROM MY PLACE.

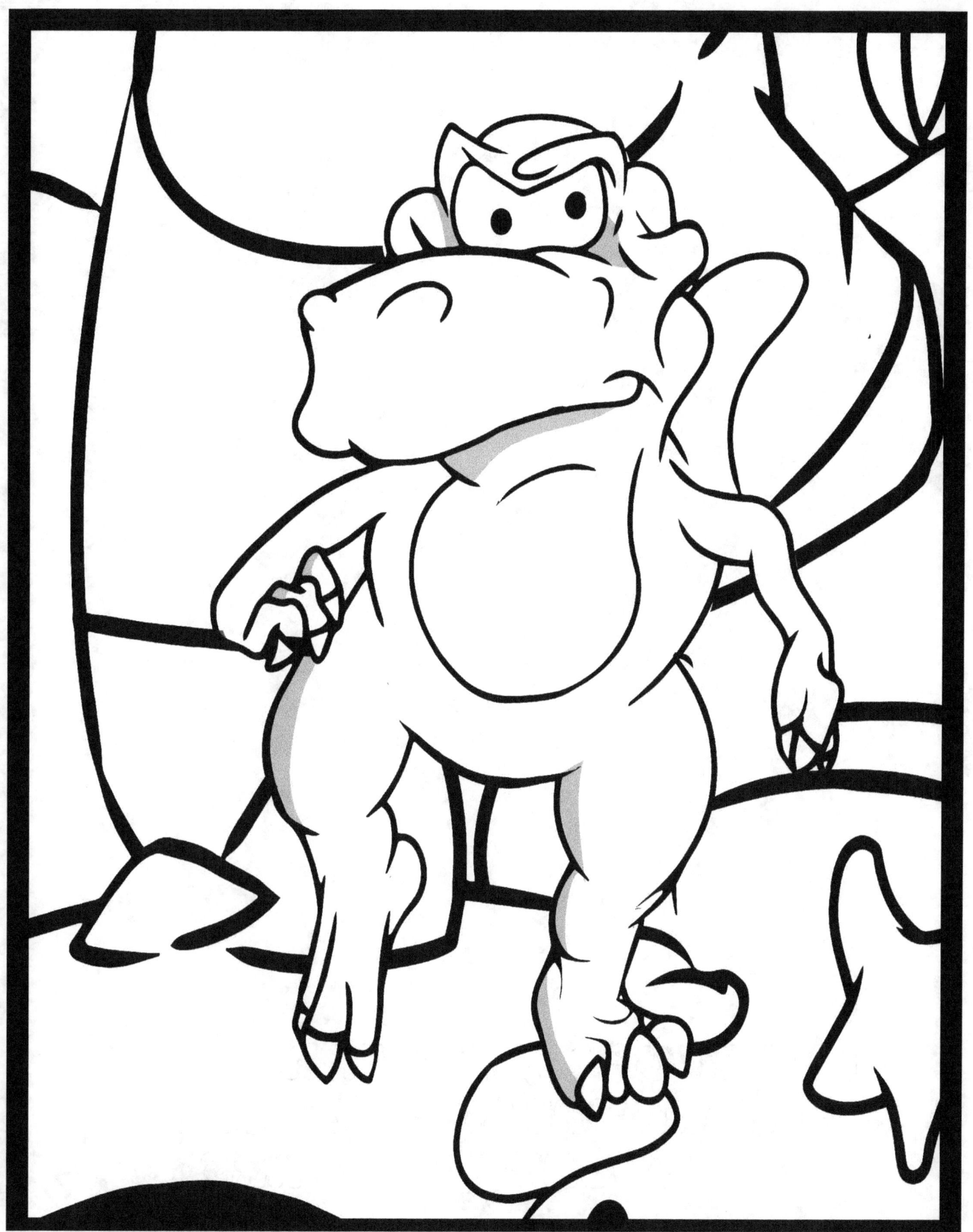

I PIKED UP MY STUFF AND I DO MAKE THE BIG JOURNEY TROUGHT THE STARS.

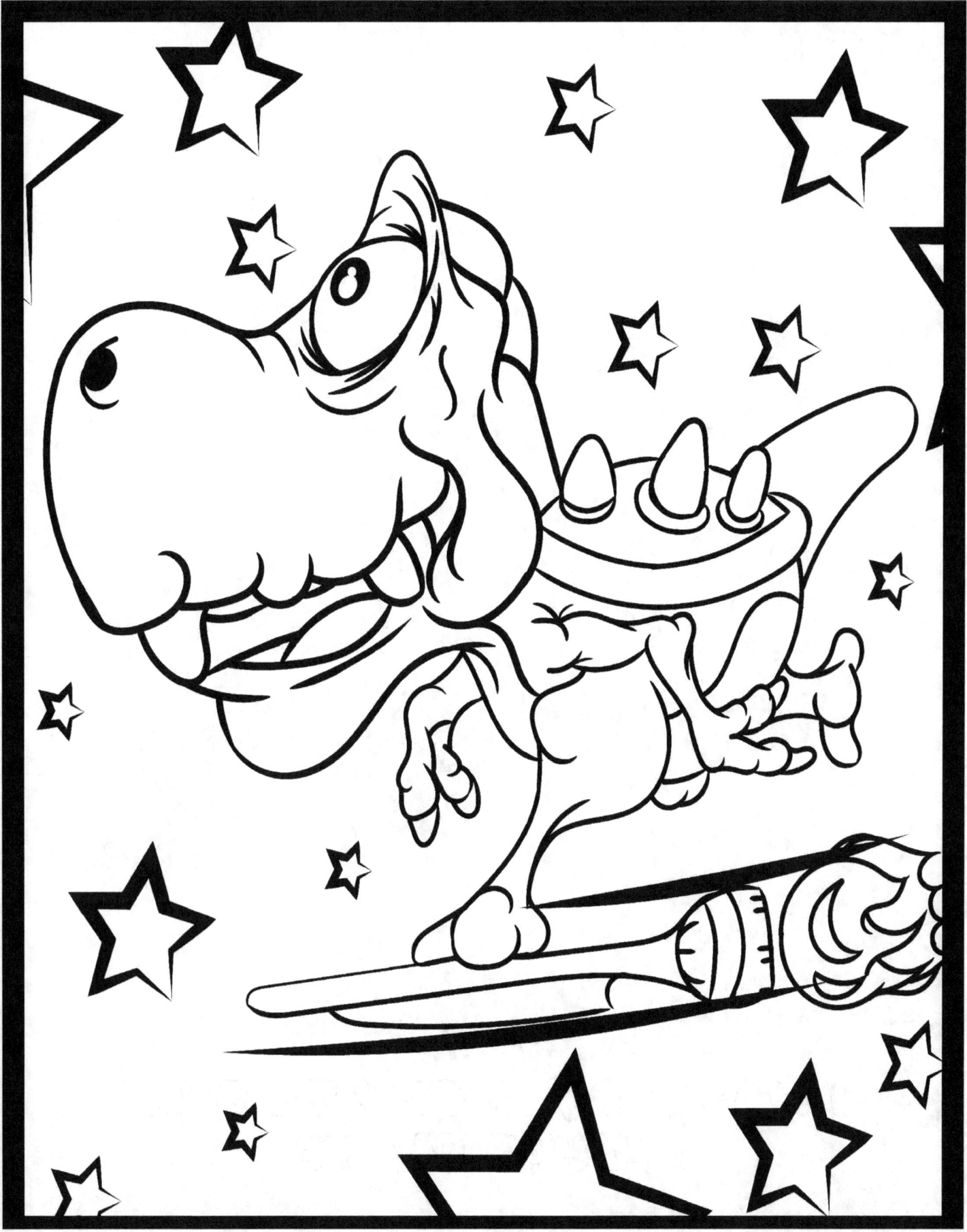

I WAS VERY HAPPY TO CAME AT THAT PLANET.

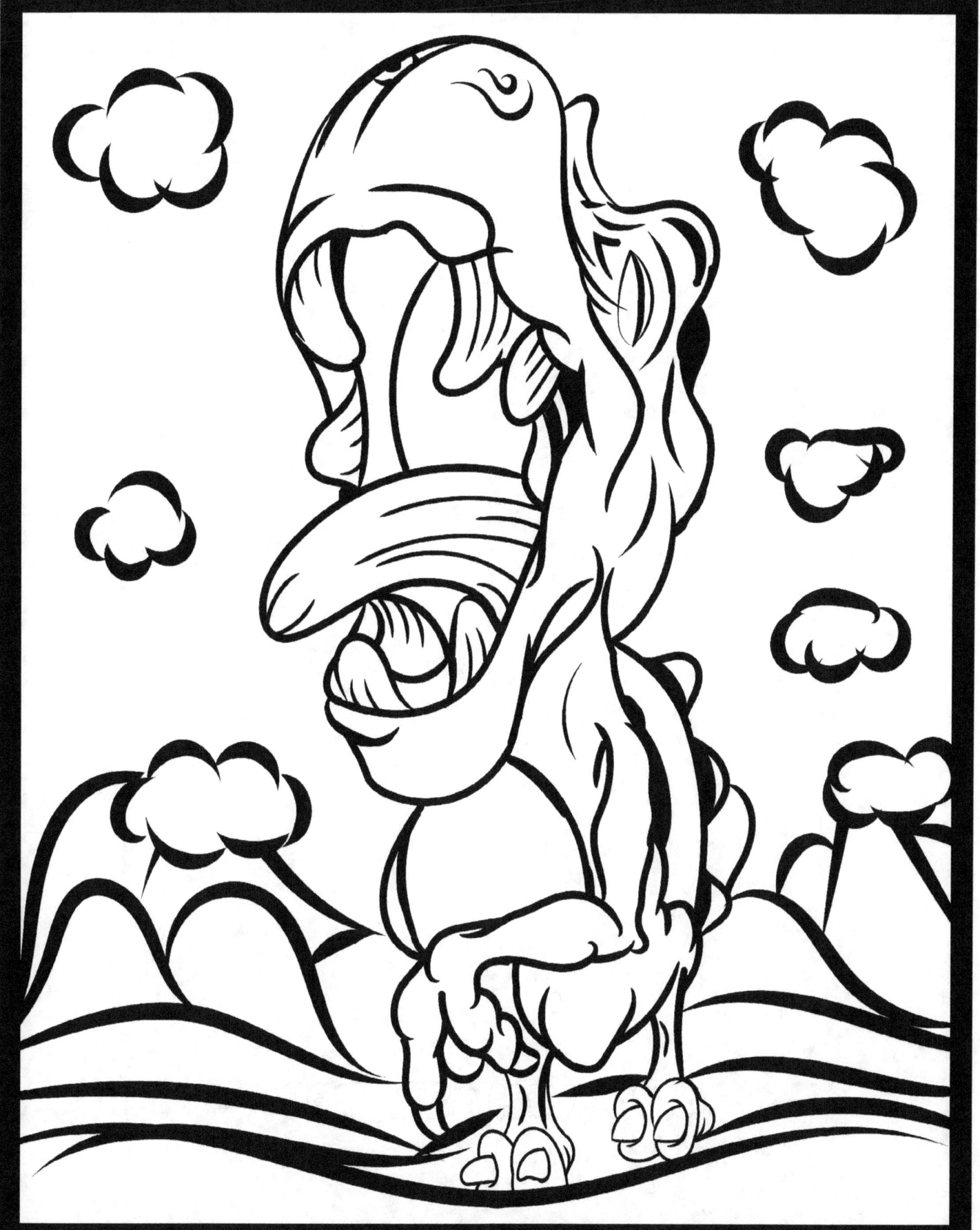

AND, WHAT I SEE?

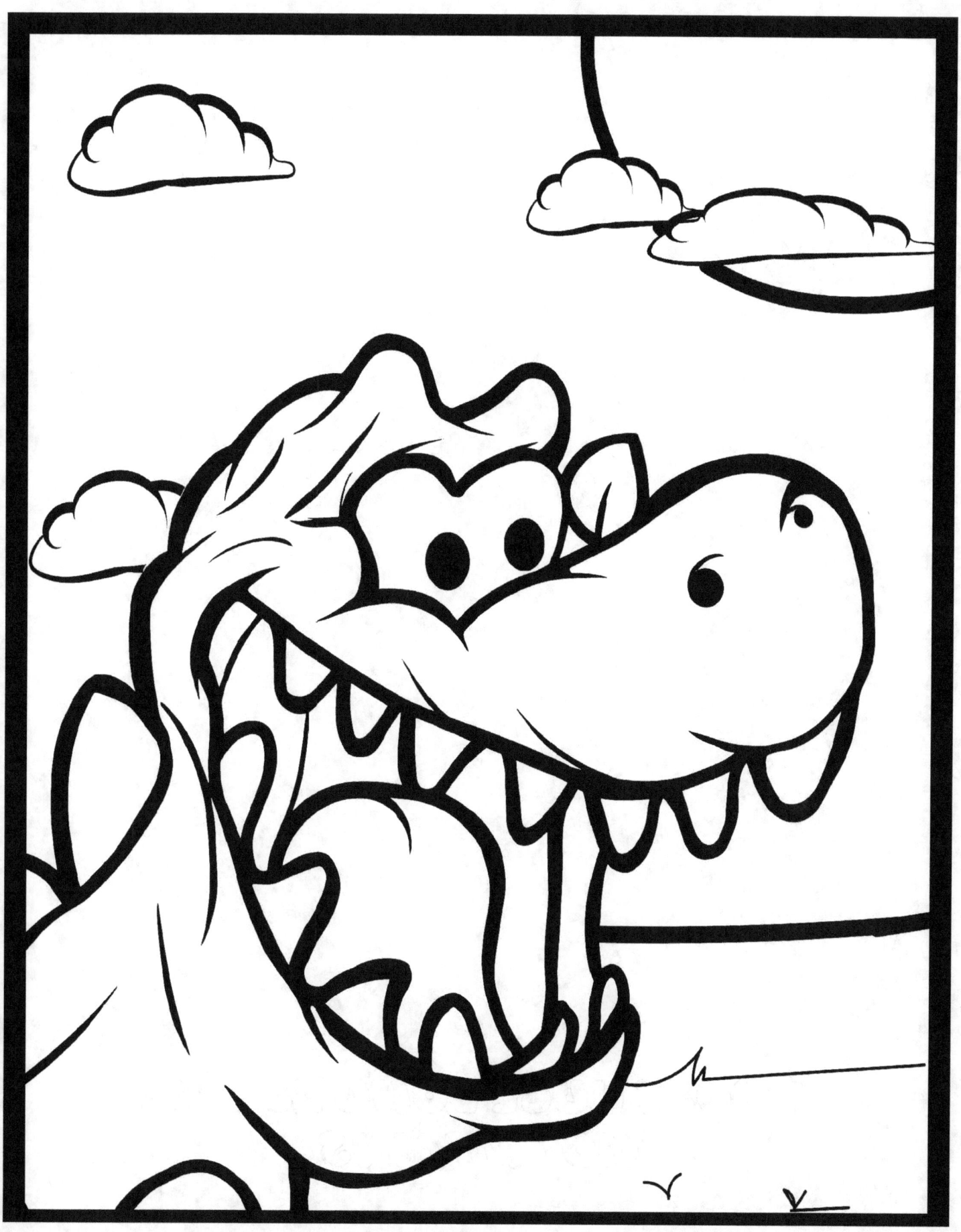

THOSE HUGE DONUTS LIKE MOUNTAINS.

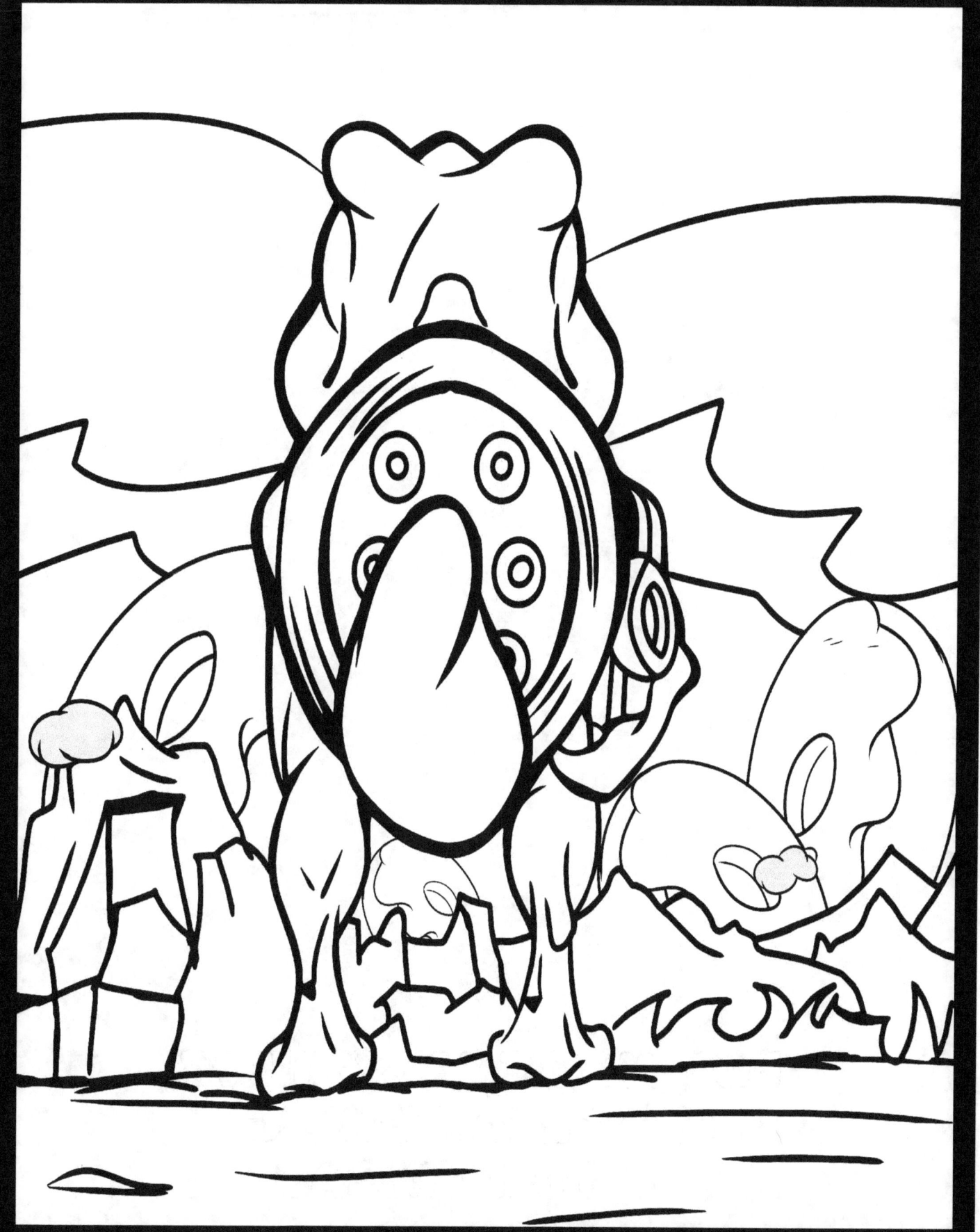

BUT NOT EVERYTHING
IS A GREAT THING
TO TELL FELLAS.

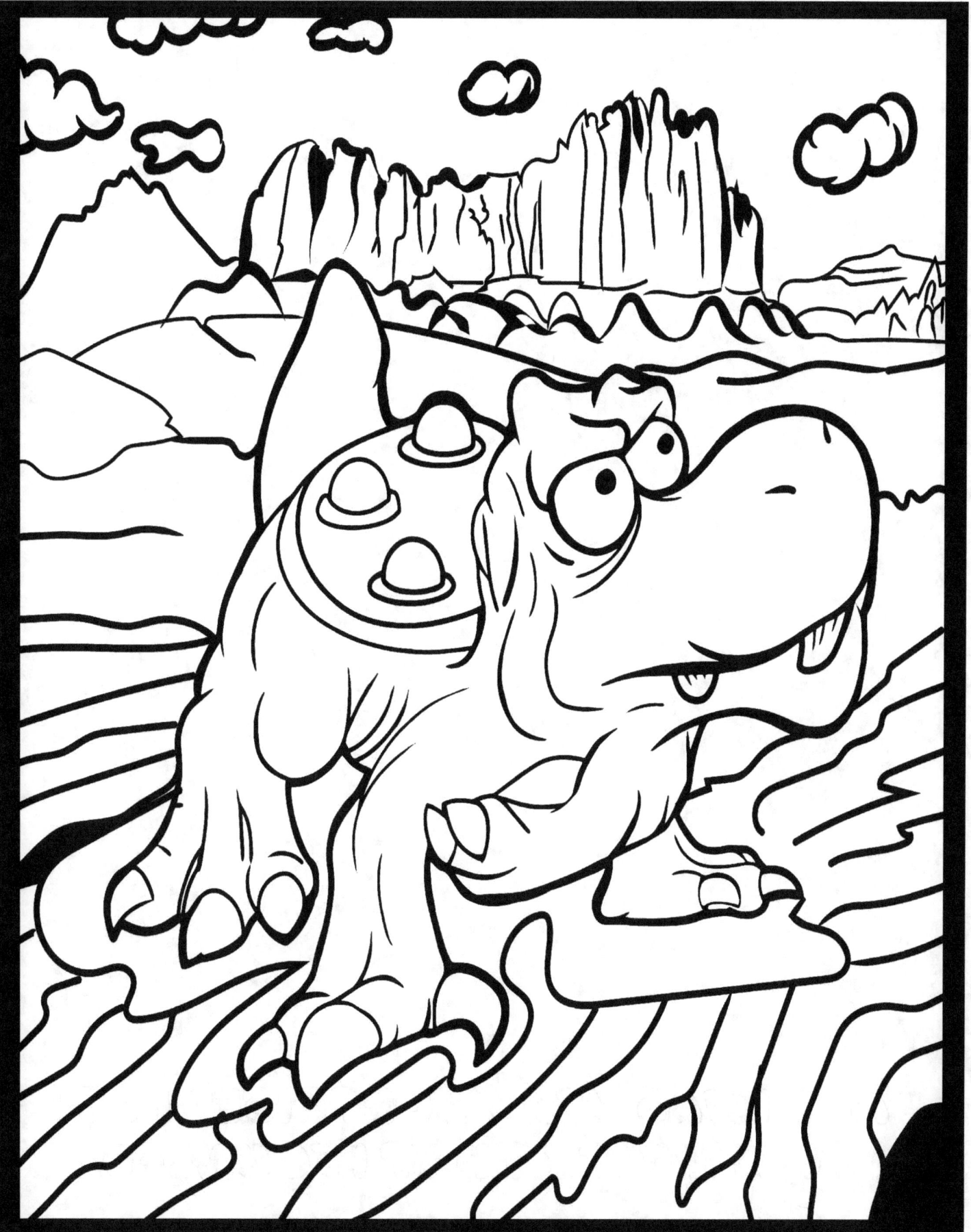

AND I WAS VERY SURPRISED FOT THE THINGS THAT I FOUNDED.

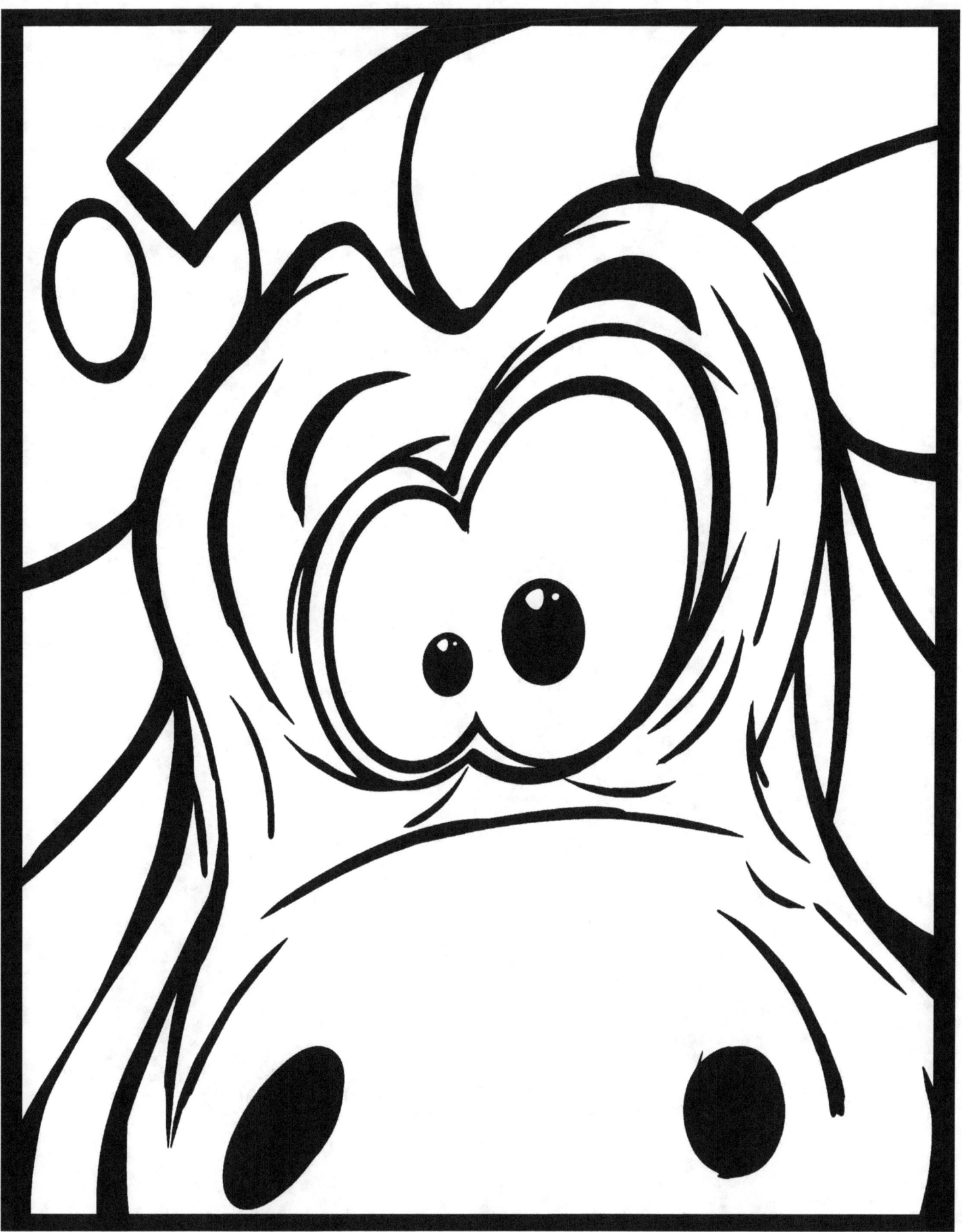

AND I HEARD STRANGED SOUNDS

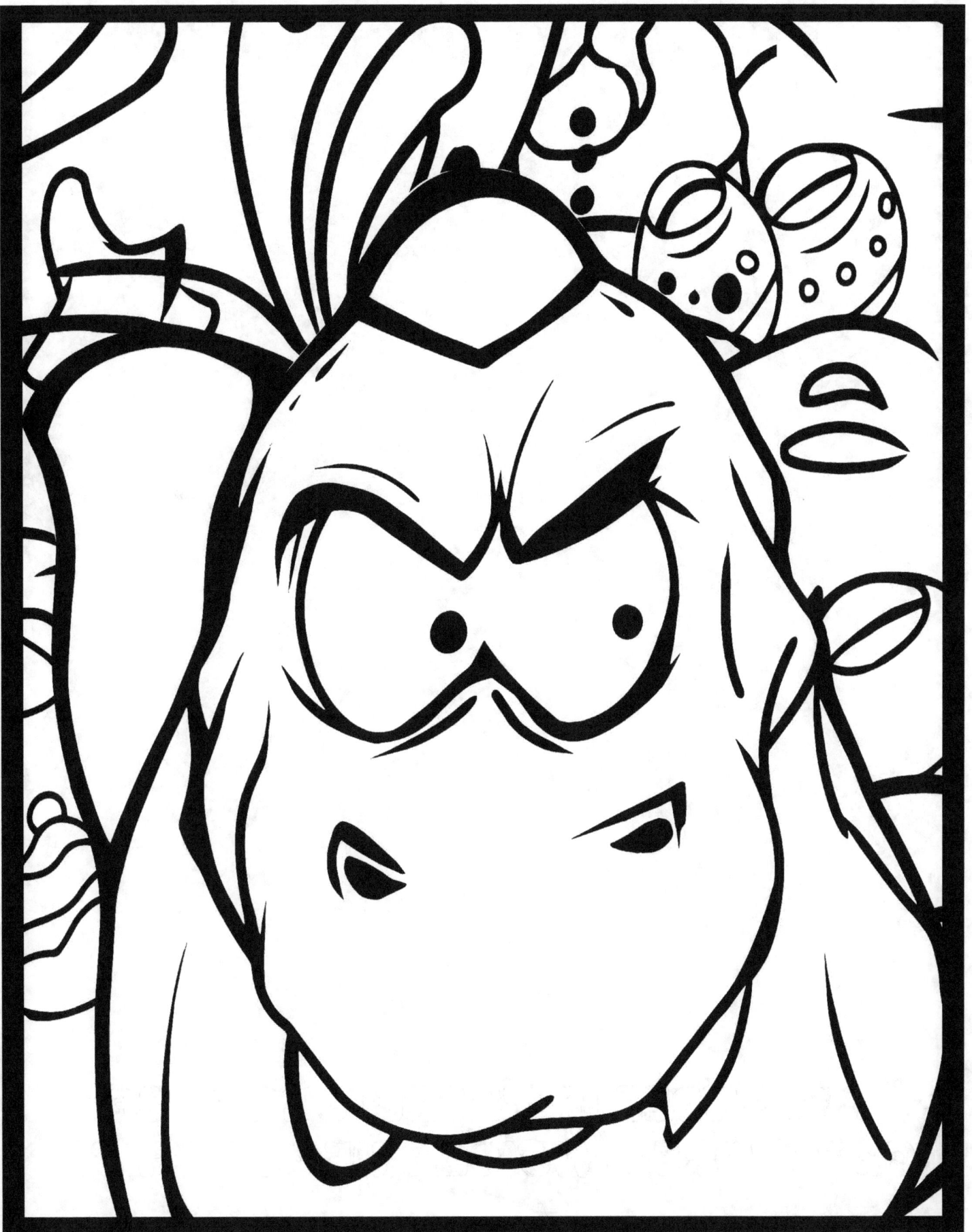

I WONDER IF THERE IS MAY BE CREATURES INSIDE THE DONUTS?.

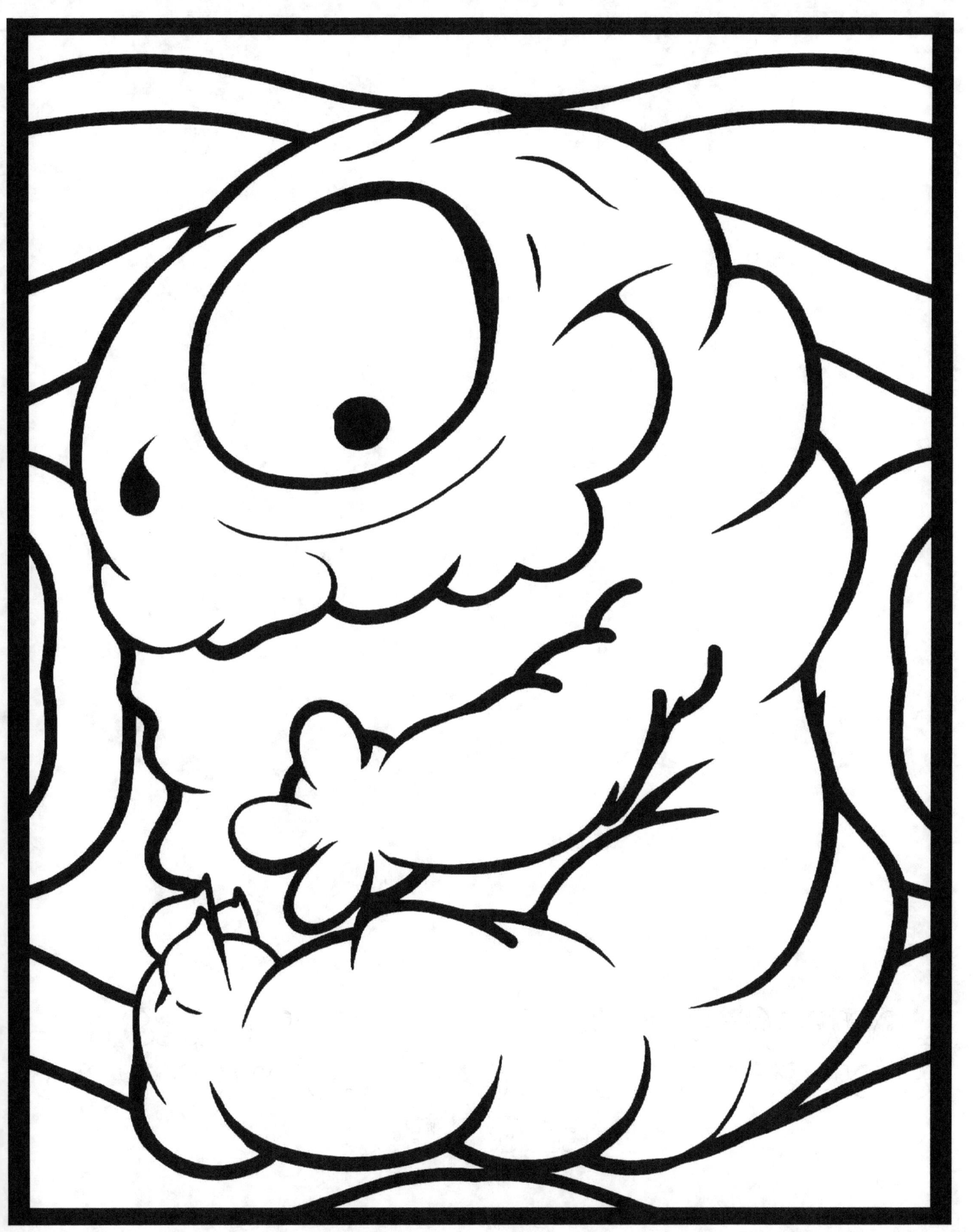

...AND YES, A LOT OF CREATURES IN-SIDE OF THEM, AND THEY WANT TO EAT ME...

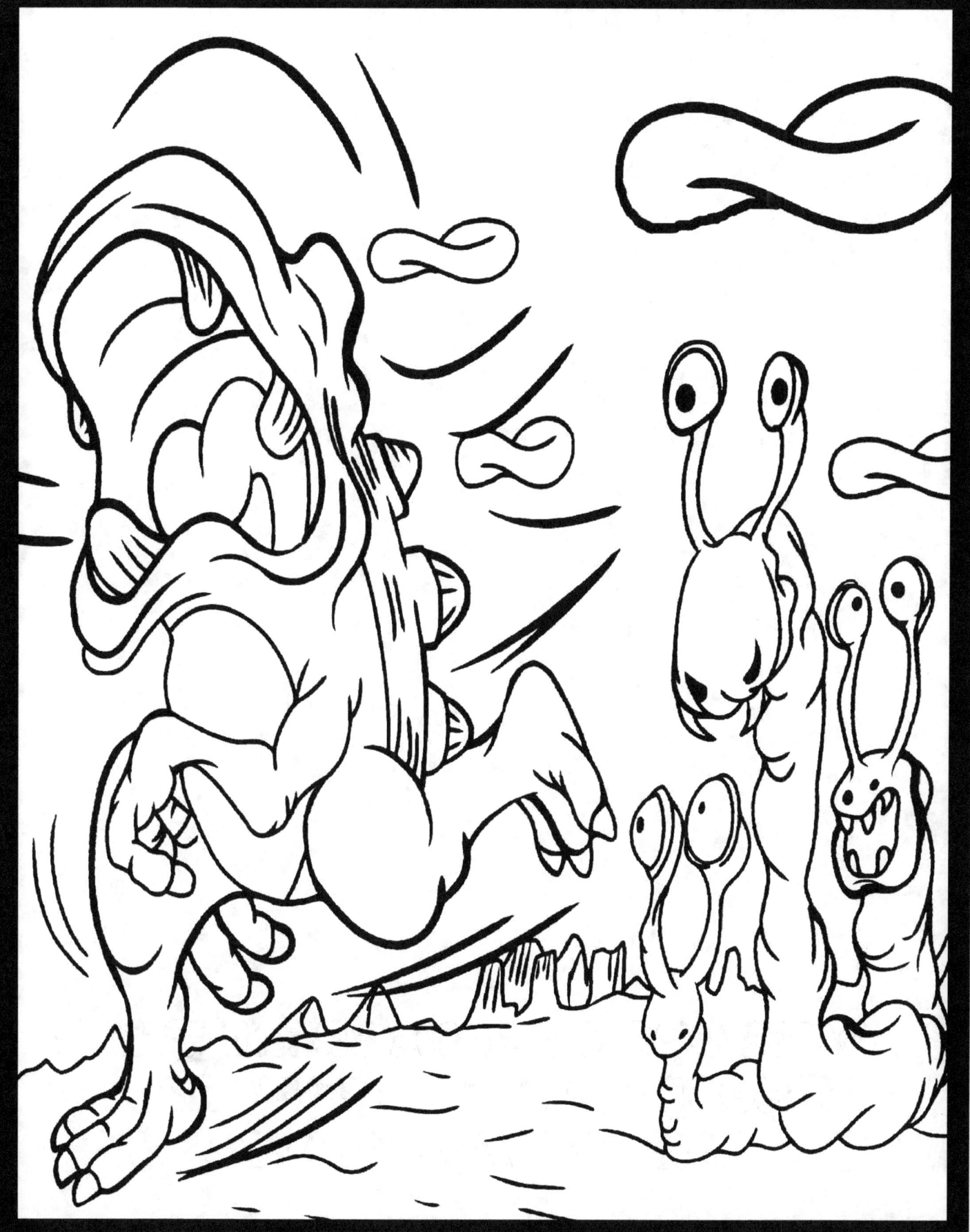

...ONCE UPON A TIME I READ THAT THOSE KIND OF CREATURES CAN EAT YOU ALIVE ...

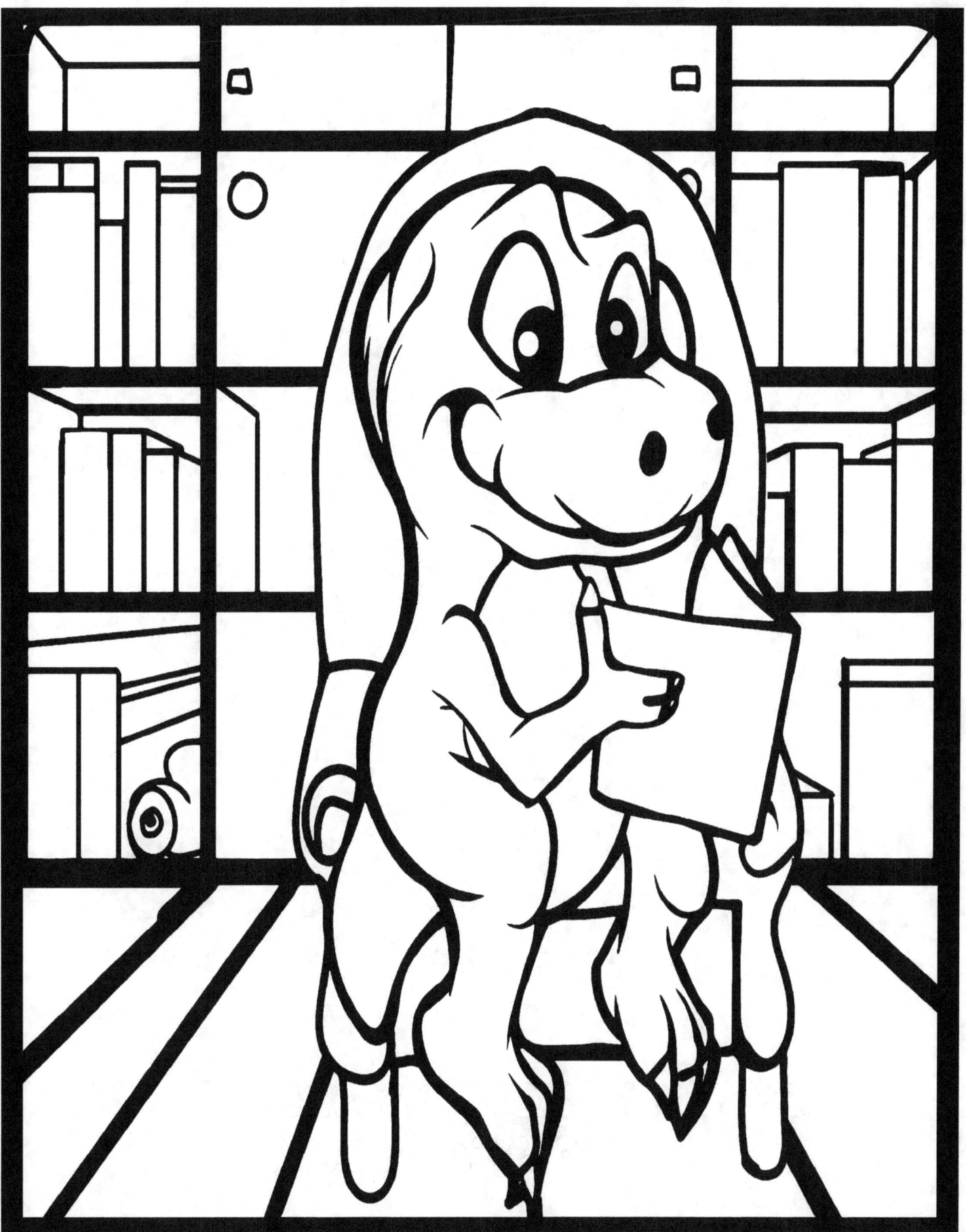

THEY CAN GROW INSIDE OF YOU
...SO SCARED....

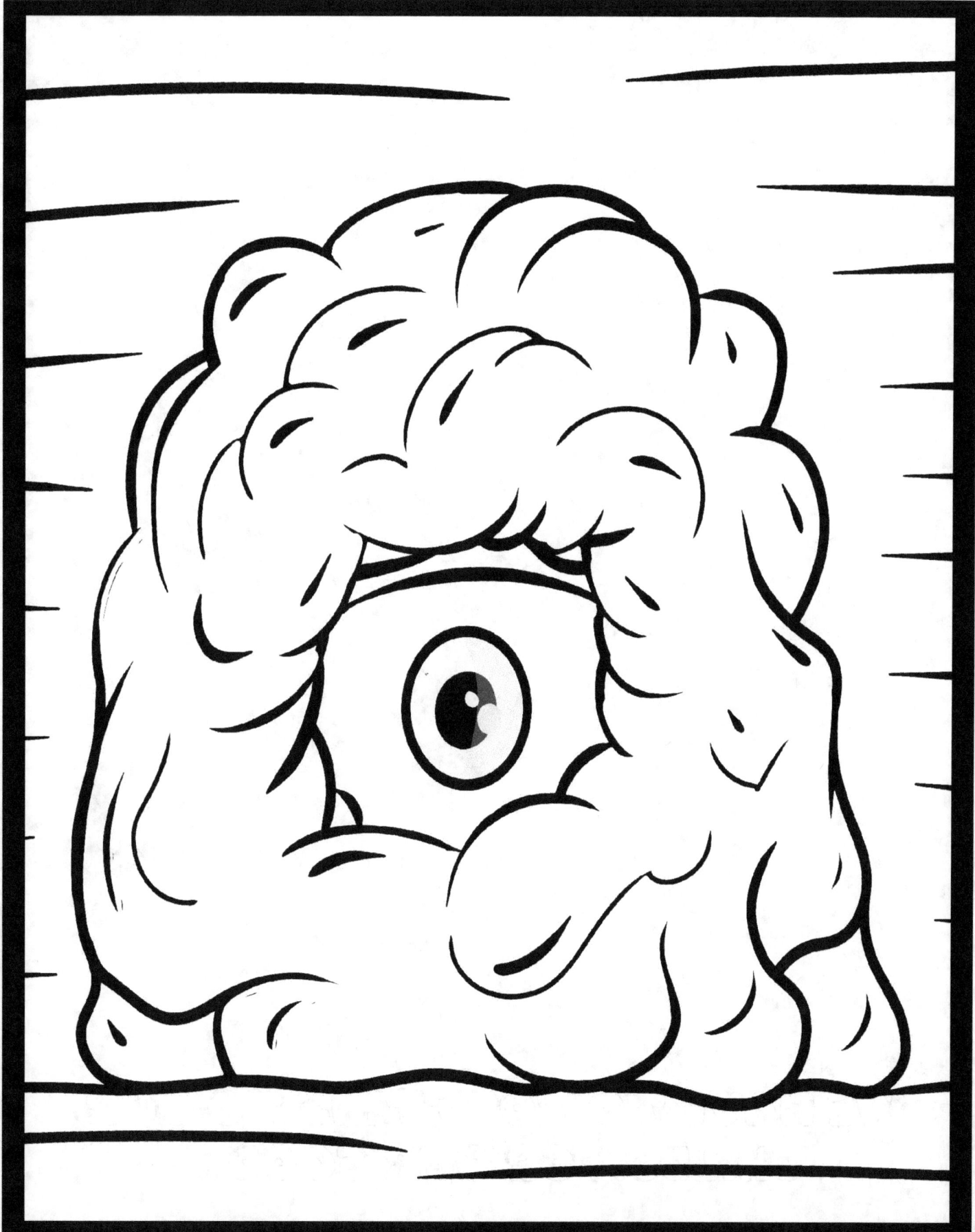

WE HAVE TO TOLD THIS TO OUR CHILDS. FOR OUR GOOD....

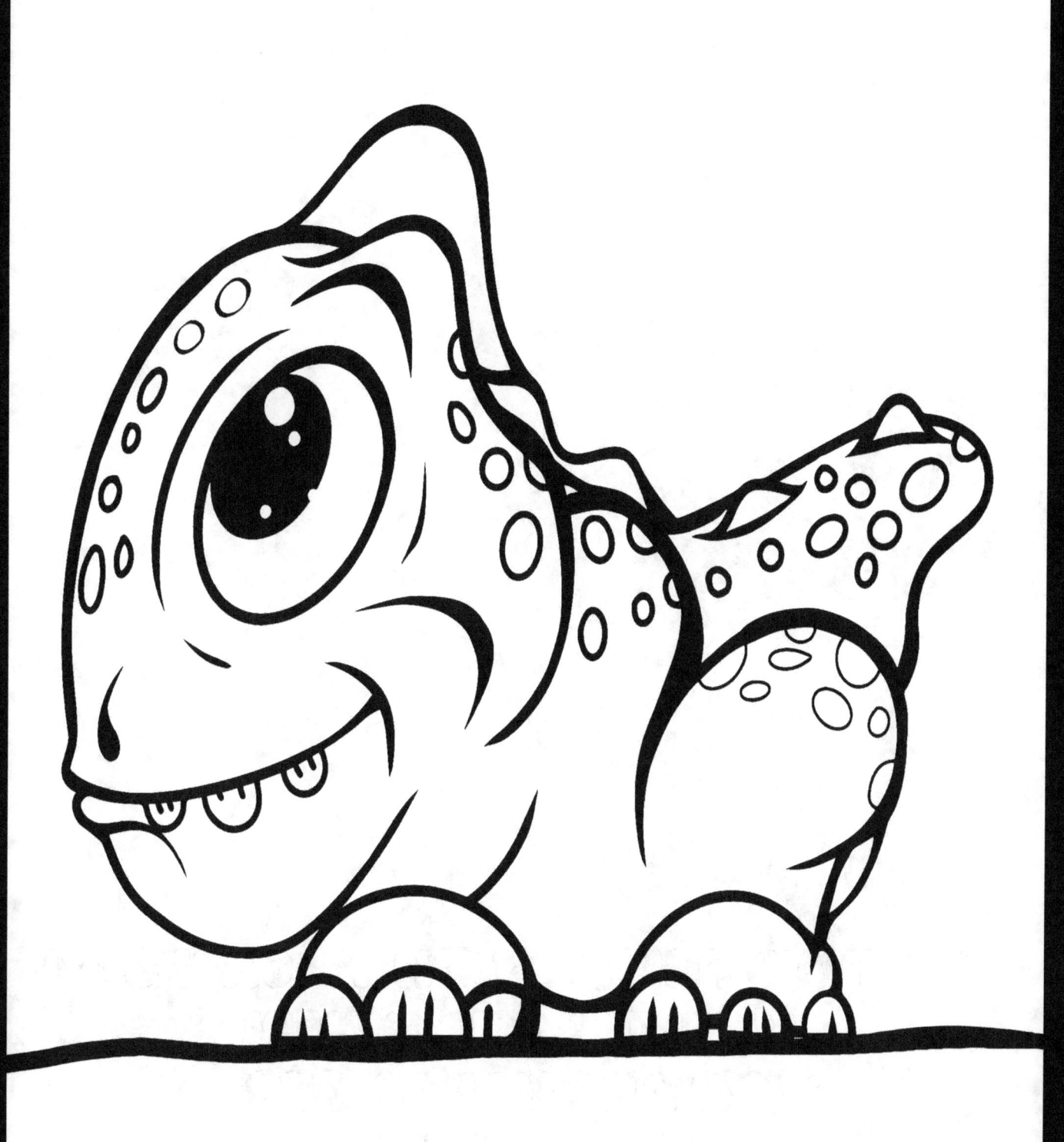

BUT FIND FRIENDS THAT CAN GIVE YOU A HAND WHEN YOU ARE IN DANGER, IT'S A HOT LAP....

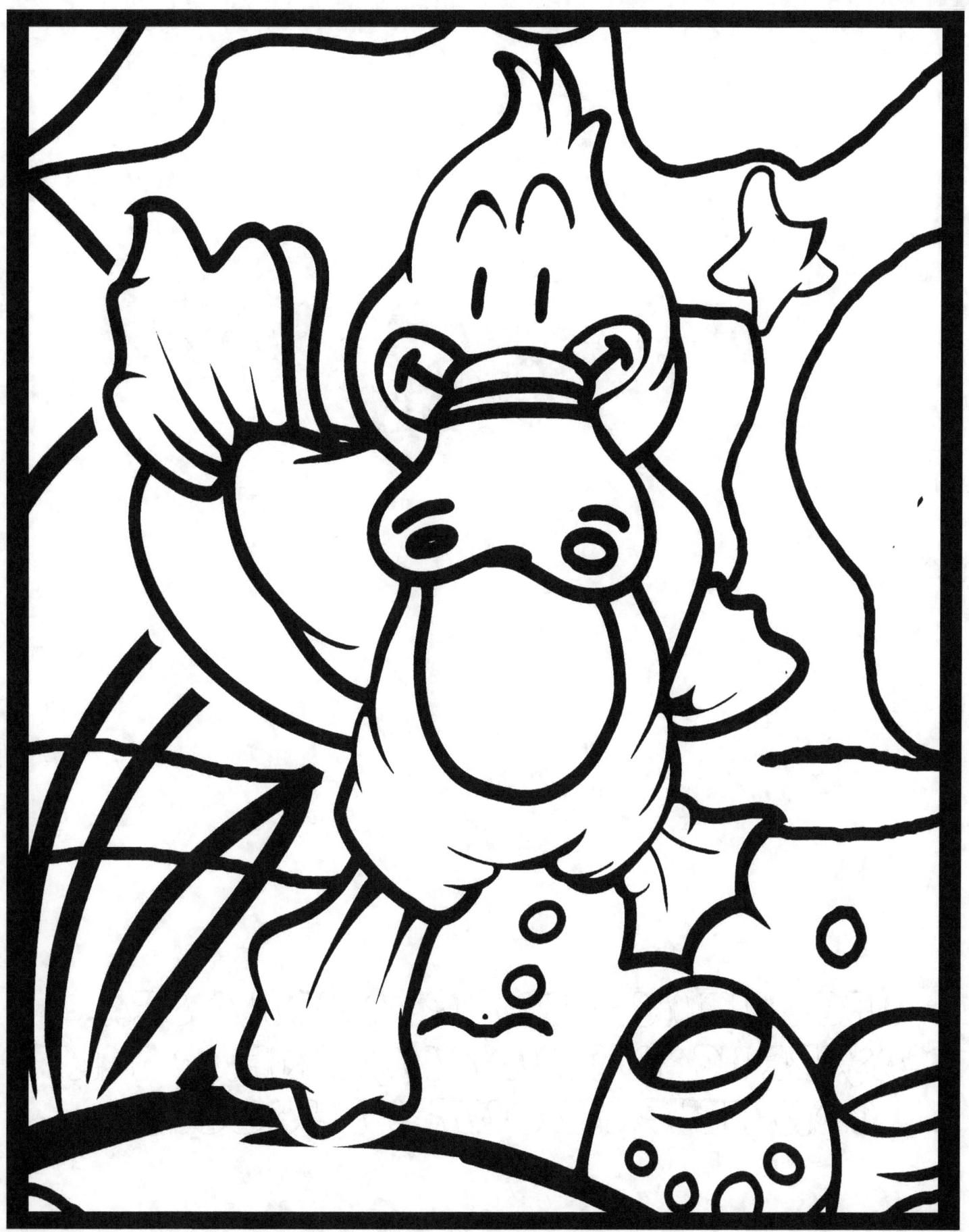

I FOUND IN THAT PLANET A SEA,- MAY BE I CAN FIND ANY FRIEND THAT CAN HELP ME OUT, I THOUGHT....

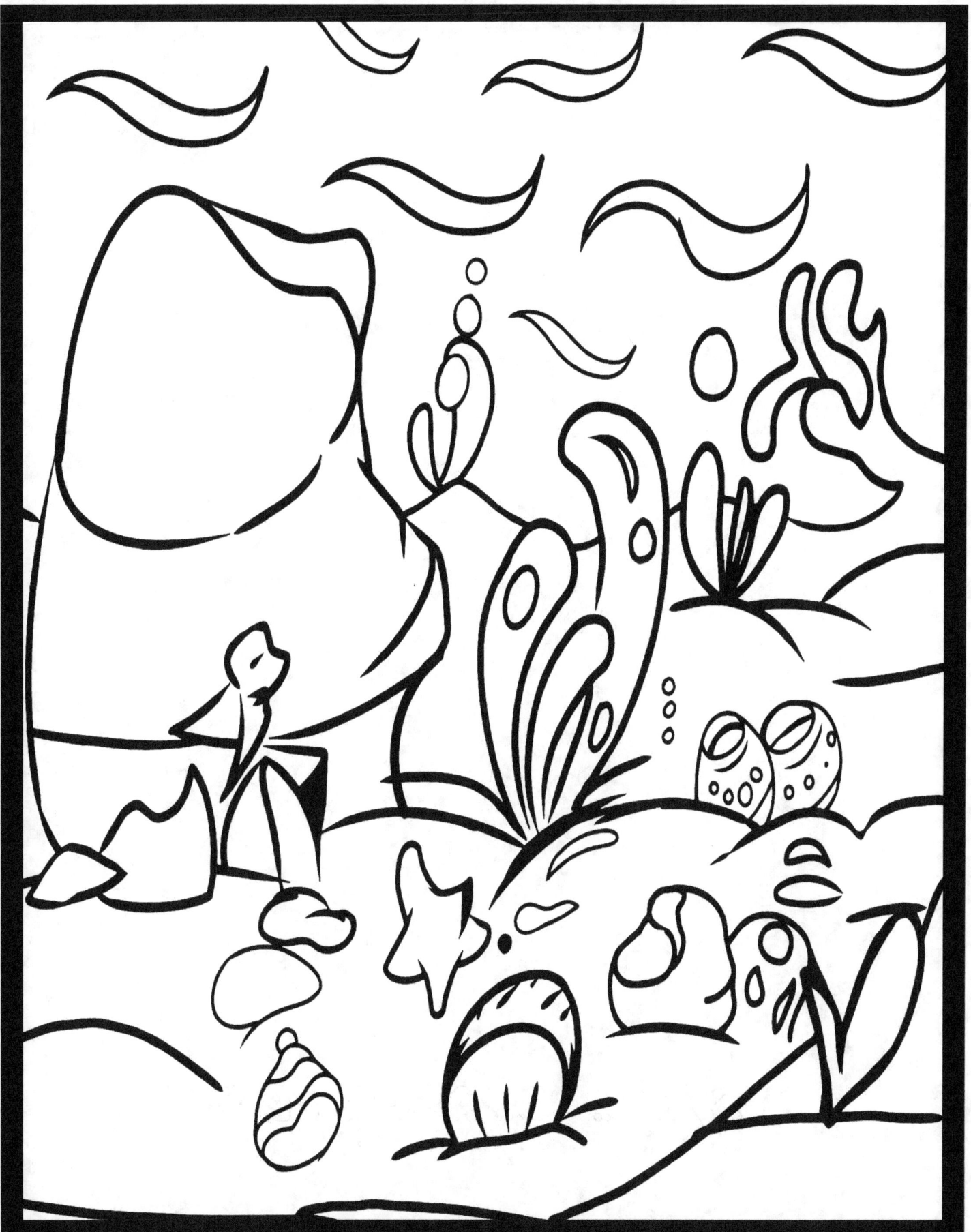

AND YES...A DRAGON FRIEND...

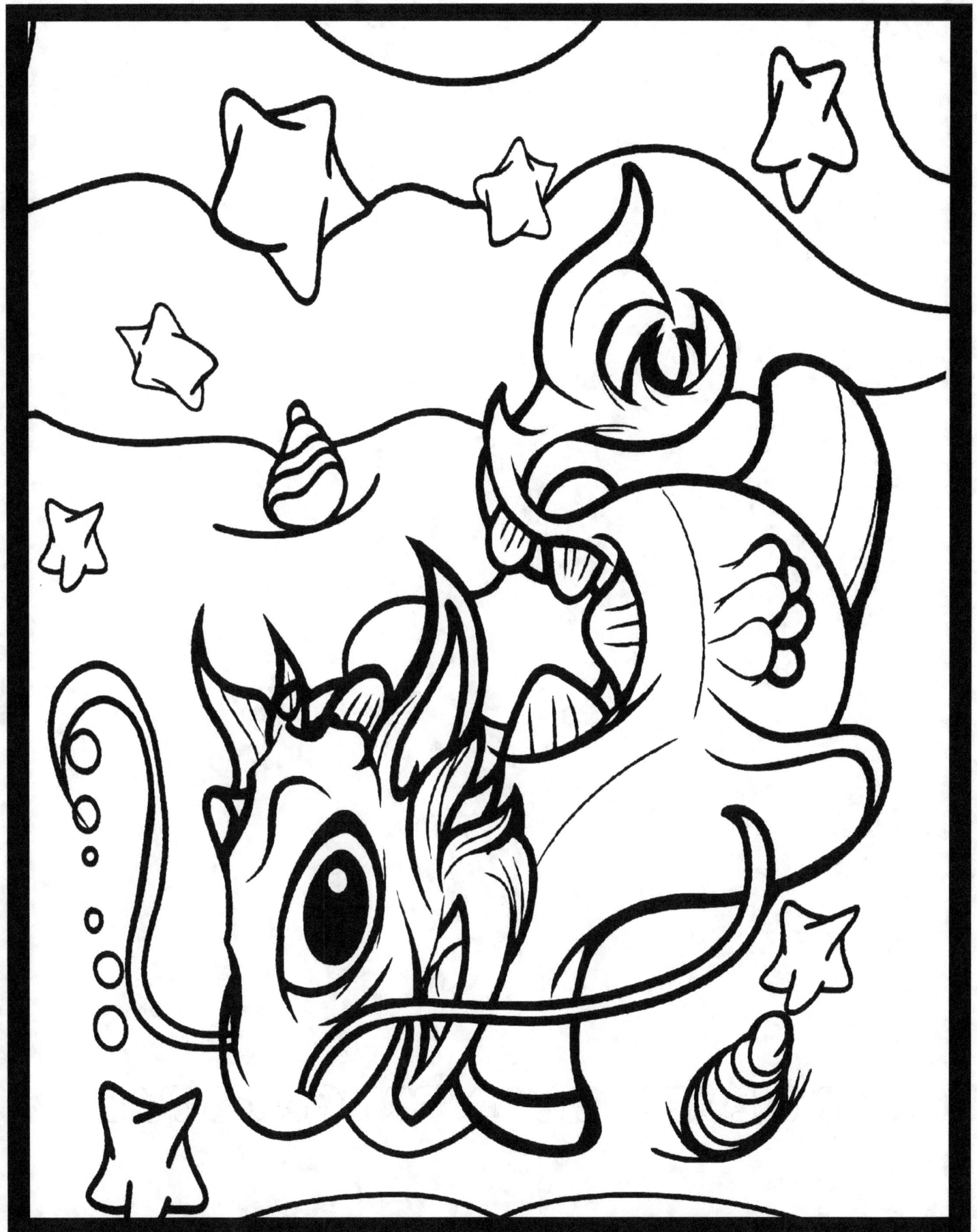

... AND EVEN A BAD TEMPER STAR....

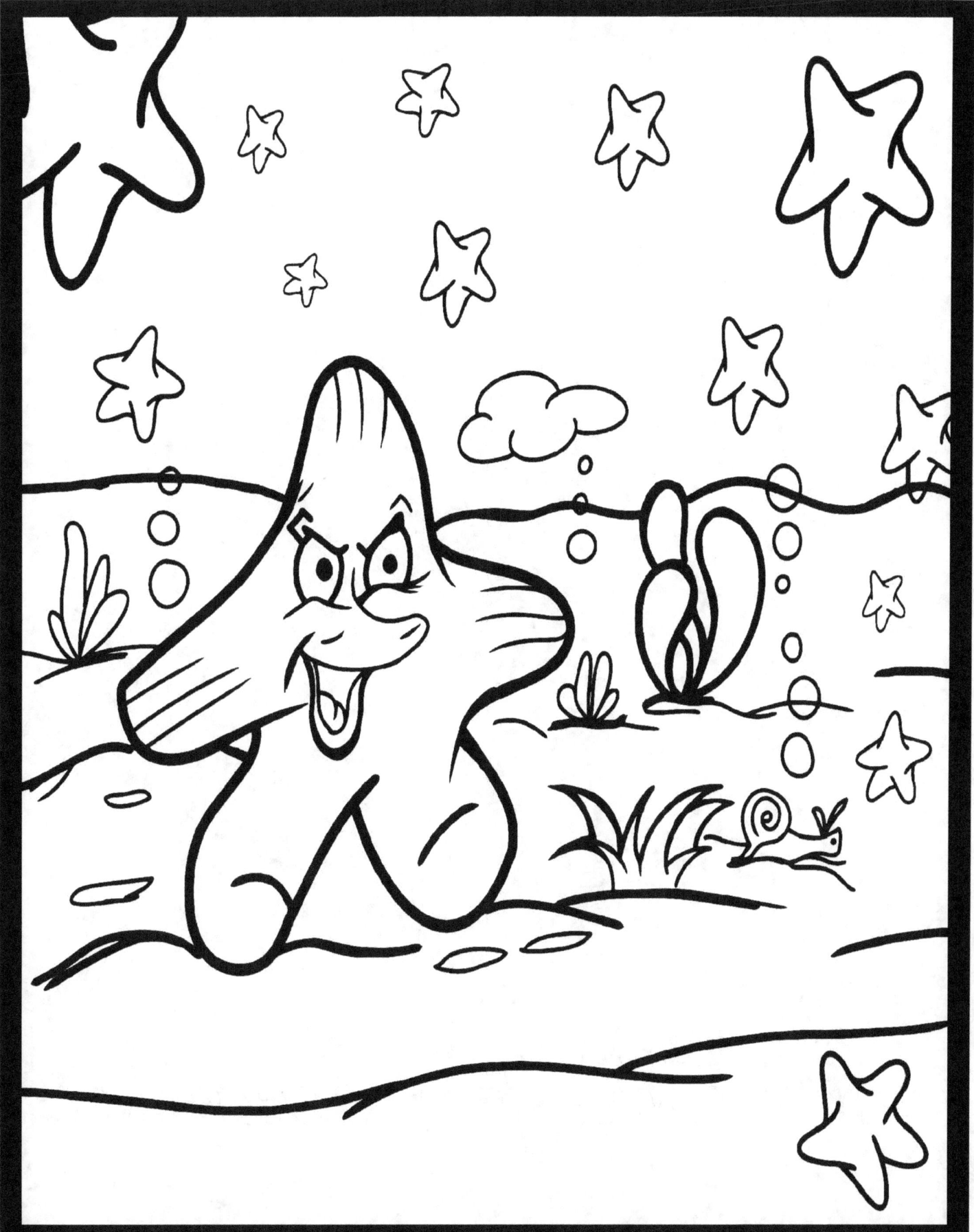

THAT PLANET REALLY SCARE ME....

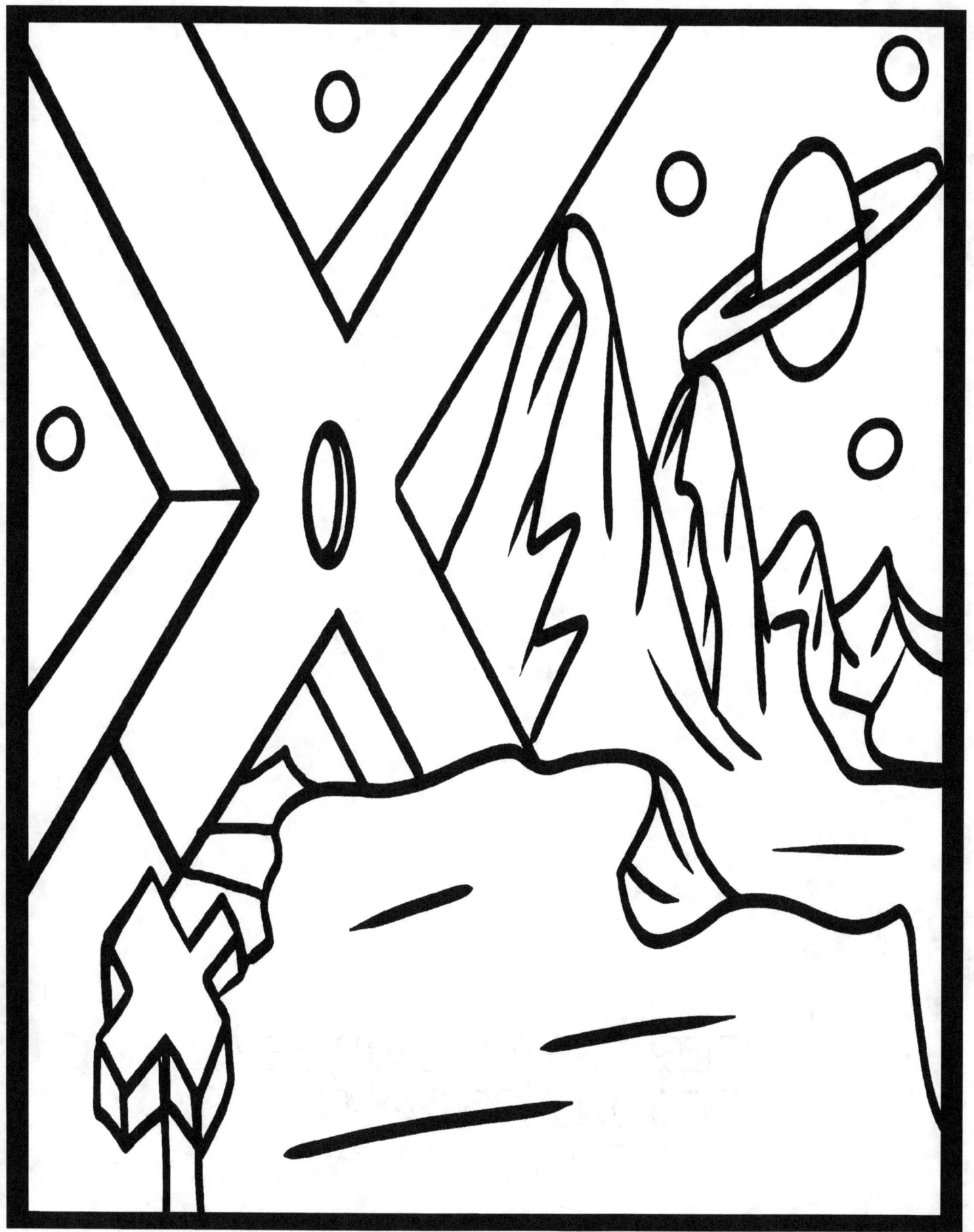

IS BETTER TO GO BACK, I THINK IS
BETTER GO BACK TO
THE FRUITS PLANET.

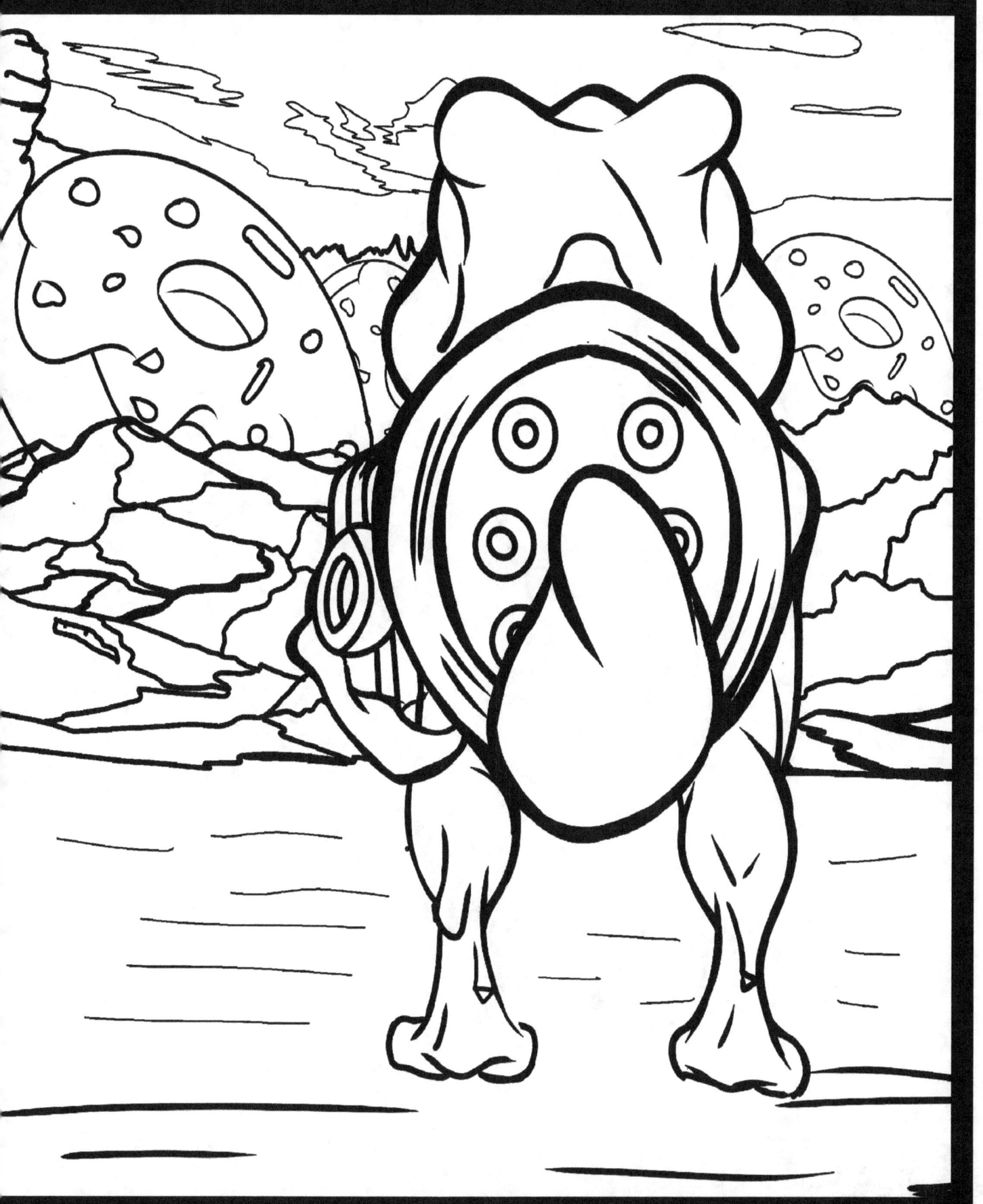

www.ingramcontent.com/pod-product-compliance
Lightning Source LLC
Chambersburg PA
CBHW080442220526
45465CB00007B/2738